Word Dances II:
Your Time to Dance

A Second Collection of Verses and Thoughts
about Ballroom Dancing

Joseph Michael Sepesy

ISBN: 978-1-4834-3663-0 (sc)
ISBN: 978-1-4834-3590-9 (e)

Library of Congress Control Number: 2015912192

Because of the dynamic nature of the Internet, any web addresses or links contained in this book may have changed since publication and may no longer be valid. The views expressed in this work are solely those of the author and do not necessarily reflect the views of the publisher, and the publisher hereby disclaims any responsibility for them.

Any people depicted in stock imagery provided by Thinkstock are models, and such images are being used for illustrative purposes only. Certain stock imagery © Thinkstock.

Lulu Publishing Services rev. date: 08/11/2015

To Mom and Dad, self-taught dancers from the greatest generation who gave me the gifts of music and dance. I only wish they had lived to see me dancing at their sides.

Inspiration

I know Mom and Dad continue to enjoy the dance on some celestial or heavenly dance floor, and I'm sure the music that's playing is "Spanish Eyes," the Al Martino version—one of their all-time favorites.

Take my hand and hold me close. Let the seduction begin—dance with me.

Contents

Part 2

Learning, Feeling, Dancing

Part 3

Dances

Part 4

The Ladies

Part 5

Final Thoughts

Acknowledgments

In late 2009, I entered the world of social ballroom dancing. Since that beginning I have made dozens of new friendships with dancers of all abilities and interests, from all walks of life—people who love life and want to enjoy it.

Those friendships have endured and flourished and have enhanced my life with new opportunities and experiences. For these gifts, I say thank you. Thank you for your encouragement and for helping me through the process. Life is good, and you are the reason, just as much as the music and dancing we hold so very dear.

I would also like to thank Mr. Len Goodman, judge on television's "Dancing with the Stars," who wrote about my book in a letter to me.

> "....I love it. So many great lines....Your dance teacher sounds like a lovely person. All the best."

Talk about old school—a hand written letter in the day of cell phones and email! Thank you, Mr. Goodman!

Inspiration

I now have so many wonderful friends in the dance community—I'm a lucky guy.

Recommended background music: "Sincerely" as performed by the McGuire Sisters.

Introduction

Word Dances and This, Its Sequel

Perhaps you have already considered the *ponderment* about *two worlds*—one of dance, one without dance—and then *chosen wisely* by taking to *the floor*.

There, *at its mercy*, you may have experienced *elation* with a *swing*, felt *the heat of a rumba*, or found yourself inexplicably haunted by *the tango*.

Perhaps you have thanked your *dance teacher* for her words about *frame*, a stance now readily assumed due to much practice, now evolved to muscle memory.

Now you stand ready, watching your teacher, the *dance weaver*, enabling you to *waltz* and take *dance flight*, or feel—actually feel—*the bolero, the dance of passion*.

Perhaps you have met that *special lady* or gentleman and seen *the dancers* who romance on the floor. Maybe you have been captivated by your own *magic dance* or a *very special dance*.

Somehow you have come to understand the *endless dances* and what *beauty and the dance* is all about—knowing *the most beautiful reason for dancing is in your arms*.

Perhaps you now step onto many floors, with knowledge of the *purity* and the *joy of dance* and your own answer to the question *what is dance?*

So now you chuckle about your many sins and beg partners with *mea culpa* upon *mea culpa*. You rejoice when recalling your own epiphanies and *inspirations*, moments of *dance-play*, and your own remember-whens, from your own *dance world*.

Perhaps you're a dancer now, planning that the *samba* will be your next conquest, and learning the *nightclub two* will allow you to celebrate ballads from your youth and the decades since.

Now, learn more—learn that to read and to dance are two amusements you can no longer do without, that these joys can be expressed together, as one, with words and music, in verse, and with patterns and steps. You now hold in your hands the key to more understanding—here are, for you, more *word dances*.

Inspiration

It was staring me in the face, my first book, and I thought, *That's how to connect the past with the present, my first book with this sequel.* Consider for yourself how to gauge your own progress, dance enjoyment, and enthusiasm, and get ready to read more in *Word Dances II: Your Time to Dance.*

Recommended background music: "What a Wonderful World" as performed by Louis Armstrong.

Author's Note

There is no epilogue that presents the inspirations for the following verses, as was the case in *Word Dances: A Collection of Thoughts and Verses about Ballroom Dancing*. In this sequel, each inspiration is presented with its verse.

Also, and just for the fun of it, a recommendation for background music is given for nearly every verse or section. Each recommendation reflects a song with the very best dance-ability, regardless of beats per minute. The connection for the music lies with the verse's title, the dance genre, or its theme. I hope you enjoy this enhancement as much as I did when making selections.

Lastly, please know that all verses are presented for social ballroom dancing, not competitive dancing, in which I have no experience.

Inspiration

Because of my unconventional feet, the concept of toe-heel-ball is largely foreign. Standing on the toes of my right foot is literally impossible, and my left foot has its own weakness. Nonetheless, Lynda and I have still managed to employ such elements of dance as rise and fall, and drop and drift and largely with knee action and illusion. This is evident, to some degree, when I dance the nightclub two-step and the quickstep, but to a lesser degree with the waltz and bolero. For this reason, I avoid discussion about certain technical aspects of dancing, such as toe-heel-ball movement. Thank you for your understanding.

And lastly, all references to Lynda concern my dance instructor, my dear friend, and my inspiration, Lynda McPhail, of *A Time to Dance*.

Recommended background music: "I Fall to Pieces" as performed by Patsy Cline and "You Can't Lose What You Ain't Never Had" as performed by Muddy Waters.

A Personal Prologue

Set Free by Dance

A leg brace, gone—less limping and tripping. Better posture—some imbalance still, but a much steadier gait.

Self-image improved—more confidence, stamina, and energy. A new attitude and outlook—life is good.

New friends and venues with new sights and sounds. A full calendar—engaging plans and new adventures.

The mirror is friendlier—slimmer image and a new wardrobe. Fresh look—feeling younger than my years.

Now, able and ready with patterns and music, a dedicated teacher and friend in a time of daily challenges and enjoyment.

And more so, a time for expressing thoughts with the written word, a time for *Word Dances*, all because of dance. Yes, set free by dance.

Inspiration

I still limp, but not while dancing. When dancers first saw me limping as I returned from the floor, they would frequently ask, "Did you hurt yourself? You're limping."

They didn't know about my back injury, suffered in Vietnam in April 1970, when the helicopter I was flying was shot down. They didn't know about my misshapen spine, four back surgeries, two neck surgeries, total shoulder replacement, nerve damage to both feet, and persistent pain. They didn't know I could not stand on the toes of my right foot and that my left foot is floppy.

I still struggle with balance—so many adjustments are needed. Lynda and I work tirelessly. It is gratifying for both of us when I conquer a pattern, a sequence, or a dance. Lynda has discovered that there are some steps I cannot perform due to my physical conditions, especially those involving the right foot. But she finds ways to compensate, and because of her I continue to learn and grow as a dancer.

Recommended background music: "No Regrets" as performed by Mighty Mo Rodgers.

Part 1

First Steps

Listen

Hear the music—take it inside and savor it.
Delight in the music—its melody and harmony.
Feel the music—its rhythm and tempo.
Let the music move you—*listen* and dance.

Inspiration

Simply put, how music affects me is a gift, truly, one of
my most treasured possessions.

Recommended background music: The song you want
to dance to the most.

The Most Beautiful Invitation

May I have this dance?

Inspiration

A dancer's simplest but most exquisite way to express a desire.

Recommended background music: "Dance with Me" as performed by Debelah Morgan.

The Most Difficult Step

The most difficult step does not involve a gold-level pattern or some daring acrobatic lift. It is not an awe-inspiring hold of near-impossible balance or a blurred series of intricate footwork.

No, the most difficult step is much more. It reflects a deep, a profound facet of one's character, an innermost desire, and then a demonstration of determination to fulfill that desire.

The most difficult step requires the summoning of personal courage, to move away from what is familiar, to face an unknown, perhaps to subdue a fear. It is a challenge to walk in a more singular fashion, to learn of and to be true to one's self.

For some, the most difficult step is a response to a heretofore unanswered call, an attempt to placate the body's need to move and to express its untapped musicality, to become one with the music.

But, in reality, the most difficult step involves the physical act of crossing the threshold of a dance studio for the first time, walking onto a dance floor for that first lesson. That truly is ballroom dancing's ... *most difficult step.*

Inspiration

Next to Lynda's sign-in sheet, there is a little card with this quotation: "Do one thing every day that scares you."
—Eleanor Roosevelt

How frequently I hear that someone delayed and delayed learning to dance. I hear the reasons, the rationale, the excuses for not dancing—I can relate. When I first received Lynda's name and telephone number, I stuck that little piece of paper to the refrigerator door with a magnet. It stayed there for six months—*six months*. Every now and then I would look at it and think about making the call, but I just didn't do it.

In November 2009, I was wrapping up my third year of intensive group therapy for PTSD (Post-Traumatic Stress Disorder) at the Youngstown, Ohio, VA clinic. The group's two psychologists tasked the group: "You have been talking the talk for years and months—it's now time to walk the walk. Each of you must think of three ways for improving your lives in regards to dealing with your own PTSD. In two weeks, when we meet for the last time, each of you will relate to the group how you have progressed with your choices and, more importantly, how your lives have been and are being affected."

My three choices were: write my Vietnam memoir, reacquaint myself with my Gibson guitar, and begin ballroom dancing. Yes, I now had the impetus to call Lynda. After that group session at the VA I took the telephone number from the refrigerator door and booked my first dance lesson.

Over the subsequent two years, I also completed the writing of my war memoir, *Once We Flew: The Memoir of a US Army Helicopter Pilot in Vietnam*. Maybe I'll get it published some day. But, due to a partially atrophied hand, I could not really play the guitar again.

Recommended background music: If you get hooked on dancing you may very well be "Past the Point of Rescue" as performed by Hank Ketchum. But why would you want to be rescued? Furthermore, you would no longer be singing "All Alone Am I" as performed by Brenda Lee, because you would now have the "Ability to Swing" as performed by Patti Austin.

Immediate Intimacy

At your first dance lesson, your first partner crosses the floor and stands before you.

This total stranger enters your personal space and holds you close in his or her arms.

You feel the touch of closed position and take your first step, followed by another and another.

You have just begun your journey in the world of ballroom dancing, and someone is with you.

You will never be alone on this journey—someone will always be close to you for every step of every dance.

Your life has just changed—you'll never be the same, having experienced dance's ... *immediate intimacy*.

Inspiration

With nervousness—even fear—marked with sweaty hands and dry mouth, while tongue-tied and with blushing faces, with anticipation and intent marked with a smile and kind words, in countless ways, every dancer has experienced this moment. Just relax and breathe— enjoy the company.

I experienced immediate intimacy on December 2, 2009, at noon—my first lesson ever, a private lesson with Lynda. We began with an East Coast Swing, "Honky Tonk, Part 1" as performed by Bill Doggett. Lynda showed me my first foot pattern and how to hold frame. During the lesson she explained the details and importance of frame, something I have now heard a thousand times.

Yes, I was nervous and awkward and misstepped dozens of times. But I caught on quickly, learned, and loved it. I was determined to continue and never looked back.

Recommended background music: "Hello Stranger" as performed by Barbara Lewis.

And So It Began

After waiting much too long, and with a feeling of something gnawing at your psyche, you gave in—you called a dance teacher and made an appointment to dance, to dance for the first time in your life.

On the appointed day at the appointed hour, you took ballroom dancing's most difficult step—you walked onto a dance floor and met your teacher.

The teacher stood before you and began instruction with a foot pattern and something called frame, followed by a basic step, and then, that basic step with music, then, repetitions, more about frame …

The minutes flew by—you realized you had been dancing and liked it! You wanted that moment to continue. Right then and there, you wanted to dance more.

You scheduled another private lesson and made plans to attend the teacher's group lessons. You practiced that precious basic step every day until it was memorized. *Perfect*, you thought.

You attended your first group lesson with people just like you—that was good—for more learning and enjoyment. You attended your second private lesson and impressed your teacher with your progress.

Your interest in dancing intensified, becoming a new passion. You anticipated learning much more and not soon enough. You were becoming a dancer … *and so it began.*

Inspiration

Large numbers of new students attending Lynda's lessons inspired this verse, as well as the number of her students who continued with lessons and then social dancing. Lynda is always thrilled to see her babies on the floor, taking their first steps as social dancers.

I attended my first group lesson, East Coast Swing, the day after my first private lesson with Lynda, another group lesson, the tango, four days later, and then swing again after another three days. Within ten days of my first private lesson, I attended my first social dance, which was hosted by Lynda.

After being seated, Lynda wasted no time and asked me to swing with her. I actually hesitated for a few seconds, but swing I did, repeating over and over again, all three or four steps I had learned.

Later that evening, Lynda's friends asked me to swing and the process was repeated—so nice of those ladies to tolerate my newness. I then asked the ladies to dance. And so it continued and continues to this day. I still look back on my baby days with much fondness and satisfaction.

Recommended background music: "I Ain't Worried No More" as performed by Mike Morgan and the Crawl.

The Group Class for Beginners

Prelude

Students arrive to music that is already playing. They gather and greet, old and new friends, introductions and chatter, change shoes.

Some practice steps from previous lessons, others with hopeful eyes wondering perhaps how their steps are coming along.

The Start

"All right, rumba class," the teacher says through a head mic. "Ladies along the mirrors, please. Gentlemen along the wall."

The teacher mentions upcoming events, the new calendar and flyers, and encourages all to attend.

Review

"Before we begin today's pattern, let's review the basic step for the rumba," says the teacher. "For the leader, the basic begins with.... For the follower, the basic is the mirror.... Let's practice that now. Ready, five, six, seven, eight, slowww, quick-quick, slowww, quick-quick, slowww."

"Very nice, now, the proper hold for the rumba—leaders, your left hand is held at the eye height of … and ladies, your right hand presses gently …"

Practice

"Ladies, please cross the floor and take a partner. This time, let's practice with music."

As a rumba plays, the teacher's trained eye assesses her students, and she makes adjustments.

Emphasis

The beginners, some still worrying about placement of feet, are reminded about the most important aspects of technique—but only a couple, to avoid overload. "Keep your head up—don't look down," she says. "Don't squeeze hands. Breathe and relax."

"Now, thank your partners, and ladies, move one leader to your left," says the teacher. The process is repeated as the feel for the dance takes hold. "Very good. Let's begin our new pattern."

The Lesson

Step by step, section by section, the dance pattern is explained. Ladies cross the floor and dance with each leader, rotating after two or three tries with each gentleman.

With surprising nonchalance, the teacher may take you by the hand. Oh, my, now *you're* demonstrating with her! But she keeps you safe and your classmates applaud your participation—nothing to it!

Content

Teaching the new pattern is spiced with analogies and examples, short stories and humor. The relaxed mood continues.

The lesson flies by, and more music is played. "Dancers, if you have a regular partner, go to that person now. Everyone else, pair up and practice your new rumba pattern."

Wrap-Up

"Very nice, class," says the teacher. "If any of you would like to film today's step, I'll demonstrate for you now. Get your cameras or phones ready."

And so it goes. No pressure, an orderly and concise process in which success varies, and your rumba begins to take shape, as would be the case for any dance during the ... *group class for beginners.*

Inspiration

In this verse the rumba is the vehicle, but any dance could have been used to describe a typical lesson for beginners.

Recommended background music: "Straight to Number One" as performed by the Andy Fortuna Production, a sultry and sensual rumba.

It's Okay

During lessons you may experience frustration. You may falter and even fail. Remember you're there to learn, to learn from your mistakes. That's why it's called class, and *it's okay*.

In social dancing, no one is walking around with a clipboard, observing and recording a dancer's every move. No one will chastise you if you forget a step while social dancing. If a mistake is made, if a step is forgotten, *it's okay*.

Stray from formality to free dance. Try something new, some non-syllabus step. The dance police, if in attendance, will not arrest you—so *it's okay*.

No one will fault you if you stumble or even fall down. There will be concern for your well-being as others rush to your aid. If you take a spill, know that it's part of the process all dancers have encountered. So brush off the mistakes and yourself. Remember, *it's okay*.

During a dance you may hesitate, hold back, and doubt yourself. If you feel inadequate and question your ability—that, too, is okay—your partner will understand. It takes time, but you will soon dance without thinking.

Don't be surprised if your mind goes blank and ...

Inspiration

Having assisted Lynda for quite some time, I have witnessed just how terrified beginning dancers can be.

They need constant encouragement, and as Lynda puts it, "They must celebrate their small victories."

For the record, in my five years of ballroom dancing I have fallen six times, during lessons and while social dancing. My dance friends were very helpful and glad to see me continue dancing.

Recommended background music: "Worry, Worry" as performed by BB King and "Thank You, Falettinme Be Mice Elf Agin" as performed by Sly and the Family Stone.

Dance Hugs

In the world of dance, they become evident shortly after one's personal space has been invaded during those first nerve-racking lessons. But they soon become second nature, as familiar as taking frame, time after time after time.

Sometimes they are given after a dance, or after some dances, and maybe after all dances. Some happen during lessons, they always happen at social dances, and some collide with the excitement of doing a step just right or after experiencing one of those special dances.

They go beyond bringing and holding dancers together—they are gentle therapy, given when sad or when happy and at times just to be close. Other times, some may speak, silently saying "I understand" or "thank you" and some may say "I love you too."

They are given everywhere and for countless reasons, some on the dance floor and others off the dance floor. Some say hello or goodbye, while others acknowledge and encourage, soothe and show appreciation. Some are simply needed. Many are just given.

They are pleasant gestures, genuine and enjoyable, but some bear more meaningful purposes, allowing arms to trail around waists or to hold hands, some for drawing a partner very near to speak softly or to whisper in an ear, and *some*—some come with kisses.

No one hugs more than dancers, so much that hugs have evolved and frequently appear in the guise of steps during dances. So reach out and hold someone in your arms—it's so easy and acceptable to give and to receive ... *dance hugs*.

Inspiration

It's true—no one hugs more than dancers.

Recommended background music: "Hold Me, Thrill Me, Kiss Me" as performed by Mel Carter.

Mixers

Once around the floor with a dance partner—it's the luck of the line. Where you stand and wait, whom will you dance with are the questions pondered. Novice or veteran dancer, somebody in between—soon the answer will be revealed.

> The ladies wait, the men wait—all sizes and shapes, sixty-second sojourners destined for one journey together around the dance floor.

Thank your partner; another awaits you. Once around the dance floor, greet and take frame, then step away—frightening, perhaps, for some, for others routine, but good practice for all.

> Partners they become—some able, float within your arms, some still learning, struggle with the moment, another hurdle to overcome.

Thank your partner; another awaits you. Once around the dance floor—every encounter brings someone, something new, an experience, good, bad, or indifferent.

> The teacher believes in this great tradition for learning and to draw upon later. Some dancers bring joy; others receive joy.

Thank your partner; another awaits you. Once around the dance floor—an opportunity to feel someone else's frame, movement, and differences, to take note and compare.

The teacher said not to hesitate and not to worry
if met with mistakes. Recover and smile, be nice, but
remember to address them later.

Thank your partner; another awaits you. Once around the dance
floor—hear new songs with different tempos and feel the music. Perhaps
it's time to adjust your dance, but be courteous and aware.

Now determine the need for smaller steps or to
really cover some ground. Employ floor craft—know
your lane and conquer those corners.

Thank your partner; another awaits you. Once around the dance
floor—try that new silver pattern or recall and reacquaint yourself with
those nearly forgotten bronze steps. Be sure your partner is comfortable
and capable.

Some dancers may take you through one circuit on
the floor. Others may take you somewhere else with a
dream dance—something about the luck of the line.

Thank your partner; another awaits you. Once around the dance
floor—it's early in the evening. Get to know someone new, compliment,
and maybe ask to dance later.

So many dancers, some nonchalant, anticipating,
others reluctant, hoping—all wondering what the dance
will offer.

Thank your partner; another awaits you. Once around the dance
floor—feel the yin and the yang. You can't know one without the other—
the teacher was right.

So many dancers, some tense and unsure, others
relaxed and ready. Remember where and when you are—
the same for whom you hold.

Thank your partner; another awaits you. Once around the dance floor—at the very least practice a couple of new steps, and at best, total enjoyment with this dancing diversion. Teacher was right again.

Two or three songs play, waltzes or foxtrots—patterns displayed, silver or bronze, maybe gold sequences. The music draws to an end.

Once around the floor with a dance partner—it's the luck of the line, where you stand and wait. The dancers—tried and true, others foreign and new. The dances—some fulfilling, others lacking. So it goes. The dancer should expect anything and everything ... during *mixers*.

Inspiration

Mixers serve many purposes for the dancer's advantage. We enjoy most mixers, and some mixers we survive to one degree or another, for one reason or another, for better or worse.

Usually three mixers are danced during an evening—waltz, foxtrot, and swing—hopefully songs with good dance-ability and especially easily heard rhythms and appropriate tempos, thus helping the least-experienced dancers.

Mixers are great learning experiences. In the space of a few minutes you can dance with several partners of varying abilities and musicality—excellent learning opportunities and chances to compare the good with the bad and, more importantly, to see where you fit in each of the dance equations.

Dancing in a mixer is almost always an enjoyable and rewarding experience. However, you might encounter a dancer who is less than appreciative, insensitive to you and your abilities, or simply not nice. Don't let it get to you. Talk to your dance friends about that if you like. Then chalk it up to experience and move on.

Recommended background music: "And the Angels Sing" as performed by Herb Alpert and the Tijuana Brass and "Around the World" as performed by the McGuire Sisters.

The Fan

Simple but effective, of bamboo and silk, for cooling the flesh between dances, and to be shared with friends.

A must for the ladies, but also understand some male ballroom dancers are never without ... a *fan*.

Inspiration

You can buy them online for less than two dollars each or for as much as one hundred dollars if you so desire. I usually order four dozen and give them to friends in need after working up a sweat while dancing.

The bamboo and silk, eight or nine inches long, are the best and last the longest. They also fit in a back pocket unobtrusively and quite comfortably.

Recommended background music: Cool down with "Call Me the Breeze" as performed by Lynyrd Skynyrd.

Dance Sweat

The body warms as the dancing begins—moisture, just a sheen, glistens on the skin. Sip an icy drink, gone with the swipe of a hand, or just shrugged away, but it's all right.

With more dancing, beads form, clinging to the reddened forehead and arms, darkening and moistening fabric, tending to annoy, but can be flung away or dabbed by a towel.

But they reappear as droplets, tracing across the face and traveling along the neck, then creeping down the spine. They are managed by sitting out a couple of songs near the cool breeze of a fan with trusty towel and are forgotten with the next dance. You're not alone.

You see, it's okay—dancers know and cope, understand and rarely take offense, share fans and drinks. Some change shirts. That's the way it is with ... dance sweat.

Inspiration

It's only logical that this poem follows "The Fan," and yes, we all sweat, some more than others. I usually carry three extra shirts and change them as needed.

I never dreamed I'd be writing any poem about sweat!

Recommended background music: "Body Heat" as performed by James Brown.

Leading and Following, Real and Imagined

The couple steps onto the dance floor and takes frame, becoming one. But their minds are far from the prelude to a dance, awhirl with more pressing thoughts, questions, and doubts, with hopes and quick prayers that the dance goes well. During this dance, both leader and follower may express themselves with words spoken and unspoken.

***** ***** *****

The Leader: *Okay, I'll start with a few basics, just to get with the music and see how this lady moves.*

The Follower: *I hope he doesn't do anything I don't know. I really don't want to look foolish.*

The Leader: *Hmm, so far so good.* "Oops. Sorry, did I hurt your toe?"

The Follower: "No, not at all. Hardly felt it. Did I step too close?"

The Leader: "No, I must have crowded you. Sorry." *I'm such a doofus! Relax—take it easy!*

The Follower: "It doesn't matter—we're dancing." *I think I anticipated— won't do that again. Let the guy lead.*

The Leader: *This lady feels nice—no spaghetti arms. I should tell her, put her at ease.* "Nice frame—you feel great."

The Follower: "Thank you. You're leading quite nicely, very smooth." *He's a beginner, just like me, and he is smooth.*

The Leader: *Okay, now, how do I start that new step? Oh, yeah, yeah ... that's it. Uh huh, got it. Okay, here goes nothing.*

The Follower: "Oh, I like that, and right with the music!"

The Leader: "Yes! Nice follow!" *Damn! Now how do I get out of this step? Let's try ...* "Sorry 'bout that. I'll have to work on the exit with my teacher. Thought I had it."

The Follower: "Oh, don't worry. This is a good song, and we're doing just fine."

The Leader: "Thank you. I'm still learning and trying to relax." *I guess my frame is all right. Nice small steps. This is a rumba—don't want to batter it.*

The Follower: "We never stop learning, especially in ballroom." *Gee, I hope I'm not back-leading, not squeezing his hand.*

The Leader: *All right, concentrate. What do I do now?*

The Follower: "Do you know the Cuban circle?"

The Leader: "Yes. I forgot all about that step. Let's give it a try." *Now, don't blow this. You've done it before.*

The Follower: "Oh, nice!"

The Leader: "That did feel nice. Let's do it again!"

The Follower: "You're leading!"

Inspiration

During a dance, such conversations, both spoken and unspoken, go on all the time. Sometimes there's very little communicating between the lady and myself. Sometimes there are all kinds of things flying through my brain, as well as talking with the lady. Several ladies have told me that they know when I'm really concentrating. They can see it by watching my intense expression.

Most ladies are very understanding and want you to succeed as a leader. When the leader succeeds, the dance succeeds, and the ladies are taken on a wonderful musical ride.

Recommended background music: "I Need to Know" as performed by Marc Anthony.

Dance Desire

For the dancer, the yearning is constant, stepping along a personal continuum of patterns and sequences released on the ballroom floor.

For the dancer, the quest is never ending, no matter the genre or dance, as one endeavor leads to another.

For the dancer, fulfillment cannot be realized, but the joy encountered during the journey serves to satisfy for the moment. Such is ... *dance desire.*

Inspiration

Is the love of dance ever satisfied, ever completely realized? Only temporarily, as long as the music plays.

Recommended background music: "Slice of Heaven" as performed by Melody Sweets.

You Know You're a Dancer When ...

General

You don't forget a newly learned step by the time you cross the parking lot and get in your car.

You really do know the differences among an open break, a crossover break, and a cross-body lead.

You can speak foreign languages: *appel, arabesque, bota fogos, cabaret, chasse, corte, develope, envelope, paso doble, passé, promenade, ronde, volta ...*

You really do want and look forward to performing routines at showcase events.

You perform at showcase events without experiencing dry mouth and breaking into a sweat as your time to perform approaches.

You know the difference between smooth and Latin dances.

Technique

You understand the importance of technique and, therefore, continue to focus on technique as much as learning new patterns and sequences.

You are complimented on your Cuban motion, drop and drift, and your frame!

You remember to breathe.

You know that nine times out of ten the answer to a problem is holding proper frame.

You hold your chest up and shoulders back, flex your knees, and understand the floor is your tool.

You don't confuse CBM (contra-body movement) and CMBP (contra-movement body position) with ICBM (intercontinental ballistic missile).

Music

You can identify the correct dance for the music that is playing.

You actually step in time with the music.

You can comment about a song's musicality in a knowledgeable way.

Floor Craft

You really understand diagonal wall and diagonal center, line of dance, and when to do and when not to do certain moves that require time, thus not blocking approaching couples.

You anticipate what other dancers may do to avoid problems.

You are really stepping out with your patterns, looking like a dancer—no more baby steps.

You automatically move to the center of the floor for a single-time swing so other dancers can quickstep along the perimeter of the floor.

You know how much space you need to complete patterns, especially those with kicks and extended arms that could interfere with or strike other couples.

You know to apologize when bumping or near bumping occurs, whether it's your fault or not.

Partners

You are as concerned about the lady's dance, her placement and stepping, as you are about your lead and execution of patterns.

You still attend beginners' lessons to pick up on subtleties that may have been missed and to hone technique, but more importantly to feel the good and bad in partners and how to compensate within those dances.

You are able to compliment your partner on appearance and dancing ability and to converse—all while dancing.

You know to stop immediately when the lady's face is suddenly filled with surprise or fear due to an imminent collision.

Patterns, Steps, and Sequences

During a waltz you remember to rise and fall, to hover on two, that creating shape creates space for the lady and her dance, and to dance into the hand.

During a tango you remember to stay level at all times, to bend and send, to display attitude.

During a bolero, you understand the dance is fluid and movement is constant, sweeping, soft, and smooth.

Head position is especially important with smooth dances, so resist the desire to look at your partner, no matter how attractive!

You place your feet at the correct angle during a promenade.

Miscellanea

You own more than one pair of dance shoes.

You own a tuxedo.

You own a zoot suit.

You have a line of demarcation in your closet—one section solely for your dance wardrobe and the other for everyday clothing.

You refer to the people in your dance community as dance friends.

You know the names of most of the ladies you dance with regularly.

You know the names of the husbands, boyfriends, and significant others of the ladies you dance with regularly.

You know which dancers like which dances.

You know what steps some dancers enjoy and are sure to use them.

You have come to appreciate music you never knew existed.

You can recite the names of the pros on "Dancing with the Stars," including the Russians.

You tell people how marvelous it is to dance and that they should not wait like you did to experience its joy!

And you feel wonderful during and after a dance!

Inspiration

Things I've heard Lynda say hundreds of times have new, more intense meaning. I'm starting to apply theory and technique much more so than just months ago.

On the serious side, and not-so-serious side, I speak much of the dance language, I breathe easier, my left shoulder continues to be the bane of my dance existence, pivots are still unaccomplished, and I do own a tuxedo, two zoot suits, and five pairs of dance shoes.

Recommended background music includes absolutely wonderful songs, such as "Bailamos" as performed by Enrique Iglesias, "Cadillac Baby" as performed by Colin James and the Little Big Band, and "Asi Se Baila de Tango" from the movie *Take the Lead*.

Part 2

Learning, Feeling, Dancing

Dance, by Definition

What Is Dance? Part 2

More than a personal pastime, interest, or talent; an expression, gesture, or statement—moreover, a personification of music, a glimpse of, a presentation of the self through movement.

It is this earth's ubiquitous and binding effect, its one, unifying language and common tradition, our planet's harmony and singular joy. That is ... *dance, by definition.*

Inspiration

This extension of "What is Dance?" from volume 1 emphasizes the individual's perspective and the much grander, worldly perspective.

Recommended background music: "I've Had the Time of My Life" as performed by Bill Medley and Jennifer Warnes, from the iconic movie *Dirty Dancing.*

Frame, Part 2

Ballroom dancing's first and everlasting embrace.

Inspiration

Simply put, there can be no dance without frame.

Recommended background music: "Falling into You" as performed by Celine Dion.

Feel the Music

The music reaches the dancers, every note touching them, every chord encircling them.

The tempo throbs, pressing against and coursing through their willing bodies, a cue to prepare.

The melody and harmony fill their ears, and anticipation thrills their imaginations.

The rhythm reaches their feet and legs, the signal to begin movement, steps, and sequences to dance.

How is not possible to ... *feel the music?*

Inspiration

Some people feel—actually feel—the music ... and it comes out as dance.

I love to employ steps that match the dynamics of the music. I'm blessed—it comes naturally. It feels so cool when a freeze, a turn or walk, a dip or sweeping ronde accompany the music on just the right note and beat.

Recommended background music: "Blessed" as performed by the Andy Fortuna Production.

Love the Process

Feel those first steps of a dance. Repeat them again and again. Refine them until they just happen—make them yours.

Build on beginning dance steps until those wish-I-could-do moments you have yearned for are realized. Then, relish those moments.

Recall those other, not-so-little things that help to create the final image. Understand each part of the whole—capture the nuances.

Let the music move and inspire you. You are dancing because of its elements, rhythm, tempo, and melody—and its power.

Appreciate your partner, leader or follower, the efforts put forth, talents, and limitations. Respect, communicate, and hold dear the one in your arms.

Repeat the above, practicing with purpose, then dancing with passion, and always remember ... *love the process.*

Inspiration

The multifaceted process of learning to dance is yours to employ and honor. You must decide to what extent it is employed.

Recommended background music: "Hippology" as performed by Ronnie Earl and "Fascination" as performed by Billy Vaughn and His Orchestra.

Breathe, Bronze

Inhale: Feet are toe-to-toe or offset to
the left, and the lady always determines
the distance. Hold your partner firmly
but gently.

> Exhale: Don't look down—when your
> head is down, your butt is out. Eyes
> to the left with some dances, but eye
> contact is good with others.

Inhale: Stand tall, shoulders back and
head up, flex your knees, no thumbs
that squeeze, hands held with slight
tension.

> Exhale: Maintain your frame. The man
> leads; the lady follows. He, the frame,
> presents her, the beautiful picture.
> Leaders, take control for Latin or
> American smooth.

Inhale: Learn feet first, left or right,
forward or backward, side and together.
Leaders, start with your left foot,

followers, with your right foot. Begin
with five, six, seven, eight, or four,
five, six.

> Exhale: The core dances—waltz and
> foxtrot, swing and cha-cha, rumba and
> tango. Other dances come later. Be
> patient.

Inhale: Time to buy dance shoes. The
count is slow, quick, quick, slow. The
count is triple step, triple step, rock step.
The count is slow, slow, quick, quick,
slow.

> Exhale: Clear your head. Let the music
> help you—hear its tempo and timing, its
> rhythm. Don't rush.

Inhale: Now, arm positions, closed
or outside partner, inside or outside
underarm turns. Look at your watch.
Polish her halo. Shoulders back, elbows
up, styling.

> Exhale: Don't worry about others—
> different abilities, different musicality.
> Sweating is okay. Take a break, drink
> some water, rest for a minute.

Inhale: So many new terms—box step, basic step, progressive step, promenade and twinkle, chasse and corte, Cuban motion and grapevine, cuddle and open break, cross-body lead and cross-over break.

Exhale: Mistakes happen—that's why it's called class. Some days are good—others, not so good. Ask questions—that's why it's called class. You're doing fine.

Inhale: Dance etiquette—spot dance or move counter-clockwise around the floor, beginners to the center, line of dance. Say, "Sorry, are you okay?" even if the bump isn't your fault.

Exhale: Converse. "Did you see 'Dancing with the Stars' last night? Are you going to the dance Friday night? Would you like to practice?"

Inhale: Live in the moment, smile, and have fun—enjoy the music. Extend a hand and say, "May I have this dance?"

Exhale: Live in the moment, smile, and have fun—enjoy the music. Take the hand and say, "Yes, I'd love to."

That's all for now. Just relax and dance, and remember ... *breathe.*

Inspiration

Dance instructors should enjoy this verse about the beginning dancer's bronze level. It presents the many messages repeated throughout the learning process. It also demonstrates maturation of the student and the instructor's recognition thereof.

Recommended background music: "Talk to Me" as performed by Kelley Hunt.

Connection

More than closed dance position, an inexplicable and elusive knowing, a spiritual hold, gentle but sure.

A mystical mingling of dancers' bodies, hearts, and minds as they feel the music, as they bond with it.

Captured and held by trust and joy, the dancers are touched and blessed by the sweet feeling ... of *connection*.

Inspiration

During a private lesson, Lynda began explaining the concept of connection—that is, connecting with a partner as described in this verse, another step in the continuing evolution of becoming a dancer.

I realize I have a long way to go but have begun to apply some of the nuances of connecting that Lynda spoke of and already have noticed some differences.

Recommended background music: Two great foxtrots— "I've Got You under My Skin" as performed by Frank Sinatra and "There Will Never Be Another You" as performed by Andy Williams.

The Private Lesson

An investment in one's passion, well worth the time and cost—and the energy. One private lesson, easily worth three or five group lessons, maybe more—it's up to you.

> "Again," says the teacher. "Don't fall onto your feet this time. Ready? Try again."

For the beginner and the experienced dancer, for the serious student, watch progress quicken and confidence build with individualized instruction and attention—the focus on *you*, *your* skills and abilities, *your* interests and needs.

> "That was okay. Now, again," says the teacher. "Get that head back. When you think it's back enough, it isn't. Shift it just a little more."

You'll work harder but retain longer, sweat more but learn more, and the time will fly with no waiting and no distractions when it's just you and your teacher.

> "That was better. Now, again," says the teacher. "Hold your frame. Frame is everything."

Personalized time with favorite steps and favorite music, the opportunity to explore new steps, music, and dances, a chance to become comfortable with one another, to know each other.

"That was much better. Now, again," says the teacher. "Technique first, then steps. Got it? Technique!"

Nuances will be realized—how important they are, and what a difference they make. Muscle memory will develop more quickly. The body takes over and frees the mind, making for better and more enjoyable dancing.

"Now we're getting somewhere," says the teacher. "Remember what I told you about ..."

Growth leads to challenges, always something more, always another level awaiting. But the teacher knows when you're ready, when to hold and when to push, when to repeat and when to relax, all toward achieving that next level.

"Yes, now you're ready for something new," she says. "Let's build on that previous ..."

Bring your calendar; pick your days and times. But proceed with caution—you may become spoiled, wanting another, and then another, and yet another ... *private lesson*.

Inspiration

I take two private lessons every week. Lynda is a stickler and expects results from me, just like any student without physical shortcomings.

I come with a notebook filled with questions and a list of steps that need improvement. The only problem is we can only cover three or four steps during a forty-five-minute session.

Recommended background music: "Where Do I Begin, theme from *Love Story*" as performed by Hugo Winterhalter and His Orchestra.

Part 3

Dances

Inspiration

Writing verses for these dances was something I put off for some time, but once I started making notes and lists of ideas, everything fell into place. I had so much fun with this section.

The First Paradigm of Dance

It matters not which dance lesson is to be presented; there are certain criteria that set the standards of class, create the atmosphere for learning, and establish order and decorum.

***** ***** *****

The lesson begins, ladies forming a line on one side of the floor and men forming a line opposite them. The teacher greets her students and then asks, "Ladies, on what foot do you begin dancing?"

The ladies reply, "The right."

The teacher nods and with mild smugness asks, "And why is that so?"

The ladies reply with bliss, "Because we're *always* right."

"Very good," the teacher says as she turns toward the men. With an air of confidence she smiles and asks, "Now, gentlemen, on what foot do you begin the dance?"

The gentlemen say, "The left."

The teacher asks with just a hint of *gotcha*, "And why is that so?"

Their reluctance becomes apparent—mumbling without the unison and animation of the ladies. The teacher repeats herself, "Gentlemen, again, why is that so? Why do you begin with the left foot?"

Realizing the teacher's set-up will succeed, knowing there is no negotiating, no appeal, and no justice, the gentlemen relinquish and speak, "Because we get ..." and adding with trailing voices, "what's left."

With a single, zealous clap of her hands, accompanied by giggles from the female line, the teacher says, "Very good. Now, for today's lesson ..."

... having established ... *the first paradigm of dance.*

65

Inspiration

This poem came to me while attending lessons the other day. I've heard it so many times, this little question-and-answer exercise employed by Lynda. It's worthy of mentioning just for the sake of its knowing humor.

Recommended background music: "Redneck Woman" as performed by Gretchen Wilson, "More Than a Woman" as performed by the Bee Gees, and "Lola, Lola" as performed by Ricky Martin.

Salsa Sensations

Quick, quick, slow, quick, quick, slow, feel the heat, quick, quick, slow.

From shores of western Africa in sad times of long ago to the isles Caribe, and a flamenco sound from España—is it salsa or mambo?

Then from Cuba and Puerto Rico to northern lands—is it mambo or salsa? Always a fiery debate—feel the heat.

Quick, quick, slow, quick, quick, slow, hear the heat, quick, quick, slow.

Classic sounds, Spanish guitar and accordion come to know, flute, brass, and strings, then the vocals.

The clave, wood on wood, lord and ruler of the rhythm, mentor of the tempo, with African drums, congas and timbale—hear the heat.

Quick, quick, slow, quick, quick, slow, taste the heat, quick, quick, slow.

During a dirty decade, to New York City; for Cuba in the fifties with a change of regime, Miami dances in the seventies, and to west-coast cities in the nineties.

Spicy rhythms, just like the sauce—a mix of ingredients, a recipe from Latino music enjoyed today in clubs and ballrooms—taste the heat.

Quick, quick, slow, quick, quick, slow, see the heat, quick, quick, slow.

A generous dance, kin of samba and merengue; when Queen Cruz reigned, showing the way to Cugat, Puentes, and Arnaz, then Estafan.

The body relaxed and loose—wear comfortable clothing to appeal, conceal, and reveal—see the heat.

Quick, quick, slow, quick, quick, slow, smell the heat, quick, quick, slow.

In a slot or moving about, shifting hips and crazy legs, south of a level frame, open or closed with churning arms.

Time for theatrics, shines, and styling. See the smiles. Time for play and a sensual chase. Bodies glisten and sweat—smell the heat.

Quick, quick, slow, quick, quick, slow, sense the salsa, quick, quick, slow.

From a continent east to islands west, then cities north, feel the salsa. With clave and percussion, hear the salsa. Spicy rhythms on clubs' tile and ballroom wood, taste the salsa. Three steps of quick, quick, slow, changing weight, see the salsa. Move and sweat, move and sweat, smell the salsa. Quick, quick, slow, sense the salsa. Quick, quick, slow, enjoy ... *the salsa sensations.*

Inspiration

Visiting Jamaica twice on dance vacations added to the mood of this poem.

Recommended background music: "Ran Kan Kan" as performed by Tito Puente and "Tequila" as performed by Buddy Morrow and His Orchestra.

Merengue

An island tale ... now a dance ... in frame relaxed ... or hand in hand.

Celebrate ... merengue ... now step left ... now step right.

Joyful tradition ... spirited rhythm ... now with hands ... on partner's hips.

Celebrate ... merengue ... now step to ... now step fro.

No set patterns ... to this legend of old ... move those hips ... slide those feet.

Celebrate ... merengue ... now circle round ... turn nice and slow.

On a ship to cruise ... the Caribbean Sea ... now danced on ... any ballroom floor.

Celebrate ... merengue ... celebrate ... *merengue*.

Inspiration

I've been to Jamaica twice with dance friends. If you go on a cruise, knowing how to dance the merengue will pave the way for a great deal of fun on the dance floor. I have noted that dancing the totally carefree and forgiving merengue comes easier than most dances, especially after one or two beverages.

Recommended background music: "El Cayuco" as performed by El Chicano and "Juimonos" as performed by Sam the Sham and the Pharaohs.

The Country Two-Step

Cowboys return from the range—go honky-tonkin'. Songs with twang from the backwoods and the Grand Ole Opry by Buck, Loretta, and Merle, Patsy, Conway, and Tammy, Eagles, and the Oak Ridge Boys. Songs about Okies and Bama, trucks and trains, patriotism—the red, white, and blue.

> Quick, quick, slow, slow, or short, short, long, long.
> At first a feel from the foxtrot and jitterbug—later the hustle and cha-cha.
> Denim and boots, studs and bolo ties.

The question posed—which way to go, to the bar for a beer or the floor with a gal? Songs about him or her, courtin' and love, rednecks, drinkin' shine, gamblin' and fightin'.

> Quick, quick, slow, slow.
> Tip your hat and smile, say howdy, and ask to dance.
> Fiddles, banjos, and slide guitars.

The answer: closed position, lady held hand to hand on the left, and on the right, arm draped over lady's shoulder with bottle in hand—ingenious, the best of both worlds. Songs from Dolly, Johnny, and Reba, Hank, Faith, and Toby, Sugarland, and the Charlie Daniels Band. Songs about cheatin' and heartbreak, divorce and heartache, outlaws and guns, prison and redemption.

Short, short, long, long.

Counterclockwise 'round the floor. If really fast, shufflin's okay too.

Big hats and big buckles, turquoise and silver.

Called the two-step or Texas two, now the country two-step—watch for capes and tunnels, weaves and whips. Songs about loneliness and work, family and love, farms and trailer parks, maybe a dog, maybe country songs.

Quick, quick, slow, slow.

Keep the lady close, sweetheart or skaters' hold, and watch for spills of brew on the floor.

Yodelin', yahoos, and yee-haws, and those damn Yankees.

Just for fun, change to a triple two-step. Songs from Carrie, Garth, and Shania, Kenny, Taylor, and Randy, the Statler Brothers, and the Judds. Songs about down home and serving in uniform, good ol' boys and gals working sunup to sundown, livin' and dyin'.

Short, short, long, long.

"Thank ya, ma'am," you say. "That was right nice. How 'bout another?"

Fringes, leather, and suede.

Now a little country in the ballroom, maybe two or three tunes a night, sidlin' right next to waltzes and rumbas. Songs about the Wild West, and down South, rememberin' when, and just bein' country.

Quick, quick, slow, slow, or short, short, long, long.

Glide and slide to a sound all its own, an American sound. "Y'all come back, y'hear?" Sing and dance along with the ... *country two-step.*

Inspiration

Since I began ballroom dancing, I have found a new appreciation for country music. Someday I'll be proficient at this dance.

Recommended background music: "Dream Baby" as performed by Roy Orbison and "Rebel Rouser" as performed by Duane Eddy.

The Hustle, for Holding Partners Again

Discotheques throbbed, ear-splitting music, the brow-raising New York and Latin Hustles. The seventies and eighties rippled with electronic sounds and strobes, fast and furious tempos—quick, quick, slow, slow.

A spot dance, a slot dance, polyester pants and dresses, and gold chains on bared chests, and holding hands—yes, actually holding hands while dancing—quick, quick, slow, slow.

Some moves from swing, some from cha-cha. Hairspray for all and platform shoes, and holding your partner—yes, actually holding your partner while dancing—quick, quick, slow, slow.

Rock 'n' rollers with scorn, ponderments—where's the melody, the accents, and where's the variety. And on it goes—quick, quick, slow, slow.

Saturday Night Fever and on wheels in roller rinks, steps called the tow truck and the eggbeater, the chicken and the pretzel, the diva walk, and even the Travolta. Still it goes—quick, quick, sl—

Then ... then disco died—a moment of silence, please.

Decades later, relived at reunions, revived at weddings and parties, and perhaps less provocative but still pondered. Still a quick, quick, slow, slow, but a slower, more accommodating quick, quick, slow, slow.

Polyester packed in corners of closets, perhaps let out for remember-disco parties, but less hair to manage and fewer bared chests. Now a less-frenzied quick, quick, slow, slow, but still, holding partners.

Today, resurrected from plastic, lighted floors of primary colors, now unplugged and brought to ballroom wood, and still just as enjoyable.

Still a quick, quick, slow, slow and welcomed by the ballroom. It's still *the hustle, for holding partners again.*

Inspiration

When the hustle first appeared on the scene, I recall dancers' excitement because holding one's partner was again cool.

Ballroom dancing has been around for generations and has survived the eras of rock 'n' roll, disco, country, and heavy metal. Perhaps ballroom dancing's ability to assimilate other dances into its culture allows it to endure.

Recommended background music: "Let's Stay Together" as performed by Al Green and "Love You Inside and Out" as performed by the Bee Gees.

Polka Nostalgia

Traditions

From Europe they came with their cultures and customs ... and their dance. Poles and Germans, Slovaks and Slovenians, Hungarians and Ukrainians, and many more—grandparents and great-grandparents danced the polka. One, two, three, four, five, six, left, right, left, right, left, right.

Settled from Milwaukee to Minneapolis, in Chicago and St. Louis, from Cleveland to Toledo, Columbus to Cincinnati, from Pittsburgh and Buffalo, to all points in between, far and wide, moms and dads, uncles and aunts settled ... and danced the polka.

When I Was a Kid

Weddings remembered at church halls and veterans' posts, kielbasa and pigs in a blanket, haluski and kolaches, and local polka bands. Uncle Richie stood on stage and played the guitar.

We drank bottles of root beer and orange pop and clowned—running and sliding on aged, wooden floors—until Uncle Frank or Uncle Al yelled, "Hey, knock it off! We're dancing here," dancing the polka. One, two, three, four, five, six, left, right, left, right, left, right.

Sunday mornings and afternoons, "Polka Party" on the radio dial, picnics at pavilions and polka fests at Idora Park's majestic and renowned ballroom. All day friends and relatives ... danced the polka.

All were in attendance—the -skis and -wiczes, the -vicks and -viches, the -chaks and -czaks. They stepped and stamped, hopped and twirled, yipped and whooped to the sounds of accordions and button boxes, banjos and basses, trumpets and saxophones—all enjoyed tapping feet and singing foreign words not understood and ... danced the polka.

Songs about beer, girls, and neighborhoods performed by Lawrence Welk and Frankie "Yank," Lil' Wally and Jimmy Sturr, some perhaps wondering "Who Stole the Kishka?" and thinking just maybe someone should, "... call a cop."

One polka announced sad news, "In Heaven There Is No Beer." But rejoicing returned with the more earthly stepping to the "Friendly Tavern Polka" and the "Beer Barrel Polka." Some, maybe with one too many ... danced the polka.

Decades Later

Fond memories remain, now outnumbering the fading realities of ethnic roots. But, polkas are still heard, even just one or two at an evening dance or, better still, at weekly polka dances, few and far between though—a time slipping away, nearly lost. Some dance the polka. One, two, three, four, five, six, left, right, left, right, left, right.

I still remember "Hoop-Dee-Doo" and "Oh, Marie," "Helena Polka" and "Barbara Polka." I miss the Idora Park ballroom (burned down), picnic pavilions (boarded up and rusting), halls and posts (now fewer and fewer), Uncle Frank and Uncle Al's generation (nearly gone). Oh, how they danced—danced the polka.

Today

We still dance to the simple and fun-filled music—one, two, three, four, five, six, left, right, left, right, left, right—not as many, but just as lively. We still dance to "Strawberry Hill Polka" and "Bye-Bye Baby," "Where's Johnny?" and polkas named for Pennsylvania and Ohio, "Too Fat Polka" and "Just Because" ... *it's a polka.*

Inspiration

Finding words for the polka poem of this book proved to be difficult until I began jotting down recollections from my Polish-Slovak-Hungarian heritage. Then I naturally eased into a nostalgic journey to my youth instead of focusing on this simple dance.

Recommended background music: "Pretty Girl Polka" as performed by the Del Sinchak Bank and "Squeezers Polka" as performed by Joe Fedorchak.

Del and Joe are great hometown boys and fabulous musicians I have had the pleasure to know. Joe and his band played at my brother's wedding, and I once had the honor to play guitar with Del and his guys at a party— just two songs, a polka and swing, so very long ago and so much fun.

E, I, E, I, E, I, O!

West-Coast Swing

Within two measures the dancers know, already feel the bold tempo and rhythm—yes, time to west coast. Untamed and head-turning, grimy music dragged in from some dingy alley, cleaned up a bit and let loose to rip across a dance floor, to arouse and surprise, to mellow and massage.

A bastard dance, born for smaller, more intimate floors after the big bands' departure, but adoptive dancers, still wanting to cling tightly, took it in. Its traits from jive and swing are most apparent—tweaked, out of necessity, fine-tuned for closer proximity then unleashed. But long before the latest decades, the west coast was a dance with primeval roots that piqued the deepest domain—the nitty-gritty of human nature.

No more jump, jive, and wail—now, more like strut, glide, and be cool. Rock 'n' roll evolution at its earthiest, the blues with drive and attitude and new purpose, but not too slow, perhaps naughty but still nice, and with its own ebb and flow through each song and the decades.

In your face, full-on, pulsing orchestration that coerces, waiting for you to aid and abet on the floor, with wicked beats and seductive rhythms set by relentless drums and a throbbing bass, more for sliding feet, not stepping. Welcome to west coast.

Listen. Jerry Lee poundin' and ticklin' the eighty-eight—goodness, gracious. Boots coaxing and glossing, poking and stammering with a shameless tenor somewhere between groaning and growling. Triple step, triple step, rock step evolved, becoming walk-walk, one-two-pushhhh, an-chor step, walk-walk, one-two-pushhhh, an-chor step. Dancers built on a sugar push; came up with swivel walks and loops; and with whips, lock, checked and continuous.

There's a bluesman with a mouthful of harmonica crowding the mic, battling for recognition. He and his harp complain, whining and wailing. They prevail and moan with every breath of wild and free, tongue-moistened riffs.

Hear the vocals. Sultry singing and raspy phrasing with veiled questions and suggestive answers, back and forth with lead musicians. Their instruments do the talkin'. Dancers do the walkin'. With swagger and flair, spins and checks, couples stagger side to side, side to side with a sailor's shuffle and step through a tunnel to let loose.

But the guitar leads, shrieking and scratching, escapes the confines of amplifier speakers, and pierces the ears. Yes, the guitar rules this new world of west coast. Stevie Ray's six strings sob, B. B. converses with Lucille, Clapton's unequaled riffs resonate, and Santana speaks with a Latin accent, all in league with Muddy and John Lee, with Buddy and Albert.

Dancers strut their stuff in a slot, find more time for expression, feeling the grip of raunchy, sustained notes and caresses of raw power chords. With tuck turns, roll-in passes, and throw-outs, they undulate and tease, pose and linger. And, no offense intended, when the lady hijacks the dance, just roll with it, back and forth, back and forth, until *she's* finished. Enjoy her sass and brazen behavior.

West-coast music splits you open, crawls inside, and takes hold of you, an assault the assailed welcome—they must dance! The west coast imprisons and addicts. Sensual sounds take you to their own undeniably unique place in the world of dance, of ballroom dance. Let your body move. Find your groove. It's west coast. It's the ... *west-coast swing*.

Inspiration

When I first began dancing, Lynda and a few dance ladies told me I would love the west-coast swing. I didn't take their comments seriously—I was too engrossed with other dances, especially the east-coast swing. Two years ago I attended west-coast lessons, and wouldn't you know it—Lynda and those lovely ladies were correct. It took two lesson cycles to become comfortable with west coast, and now I love it. And by the way, Lynda and the ladies never let me forget about my initial position and subsequent conversion.

Recommended background music: "Alone in the Dark" as performed by John Hiatt—guitar at its grimiest, from the movie *True Lies* when Jamie Lee Curtis dances for Arnold Schwarzenegger—and "Night Train" as performed by Boots Randolf, saxophone satisfaction guaranteed.

Love the Tango, Hate the Tango

The Tango, Part 2

By its birth and nature, by its place and repute, the tango defies and stands alone. Singular in count and out of step with other dances, the tango has found its place in the world of ballroom dancing. But beware, sometimes it can become a dancer's personal purgatory.

For the Dancer

The tango delights, yet it can bewilder. It can placate and satisfy then frustrate and abandon. The tango can enhance or embarrass, embrace or scorn!

The tango can sustain or unbalance a dancer. It can prevail and welcome. It can dismiss then forget. The tango can possess you. It can squander you!

It challenges and then, in triumph, sharpens technique and touch, but it can discourage and dull, defeating such methods and gains. Come here—get away from me! Make it stop—dance another!

To the Senses

The tango is soft moonlight, a vision to behold. It is blinding, harsh sunlight, causing one to look away.

Its music can be frenzied, a cacophony with screeching violins and wild syncopation. Its sound can soothe and quell with mellow guitars and the bandoneon.

The tango can be delicious or bittersweet, tart but never bland. It can be savored or spat out!

The tango strips a dancer bare and chills to the bone. It can wrap a body in affection and warmth.

The tango envelops, sedates, and intoxicates with an alluring scent. It can smother and choke. History or myth, legend or fact suggests the tango can stink!

To the Psyche

The tango can cherish or deny the dancer. It seduces then betrays, treasures then rejects. The tango can build or crush one's confidence. It can create or destroy a persona. The tango encourages. It can insult!

The tango can wound the pride or bestow esteem. It can devastate a desire or sate a hunger. It can be spiteful and brutal, breaking the heart and bruising the ego. It is romantic and sensual, warming the heart and arousing lust!

Onto Itself

The tango appears on the floor, a flickering candle's flame or a blazing inferno, a surreal, misty wisp or foreboding, eerie darkness.

Its steps are smooth and gentle yet powerful. A peaceful moment, then sharp, fiery, and fierce—a belligerent encounter!

The tango is purity and chaos, consent or taboo. It is true—it respects and gives, but it can lie, cheat, and waste!

The tango is an adventure, never routine. It can be an enigma or an answer. It is the yin and the yang, the calm and the storm, the blossom and the thorn. It is the beauty and the beast!

The Paradox for Ponderment

The tango has been enjoyed and reviled; it is amazing and enchanting or, perhaps, deceiving and shocking. At times it is a loving dance, endearing to all. Other times it is an angry dance detesting all!

The tango will never be understood, never be tamed. It will taunt and trouble, try and trample. It will promise and hold, lull and comfort—an ever-changing contradiction.

Perhaps the tango is loved, just for a while. Perhaps the tango is hated, just for a while. But when all is experienced and considered, one thing is certain—we must dance the tango!

I *love the tango*. I *hate the tango*!

Inspiration

I suspect this verse may raise an eyebrow or two. I also suspect that some dancers, perhaps more than not, will relate to its message. I have found that with each pattern, technique, and step ever attempted, each dance or routine ever performed, one or the other analogy or any descriptor can be applied.

Recommended background music: "La Cumparsita" as performed by Billy Vaughn and His Orchestra, the best version of this classic tango I have ever heard, and "Nights in Argentina" as performed by Latin Music Club.

Swing, Part 2

Triple step, triple step, rock step.
You take the rock, and I'll take the roll.
Triple step, triple step, rock step.

Inspiration

The swing is so much fun! Take your pick—east coast, west coast, or single-time.

Recommended background music: "Blues in the Night" as performed by Quincy Jones and His Orchestra, "Chattanooga Choo Choo" as performed by Glenn Miller, "Rocket to the Moon" as performed by Colin James, and "Walk of Shame" as performed by Eight to the Bar.

The Quickstep, Part 2

Don't think. There isn't time—it's *the quickstep*!

Inspiration

In March 2014, I danced a routine with Lynda and three other couples in a benefit performance for a local charity. The routine consisted of the quickstep, Charleston, and single-time swing. It was the most difficult dance I had ever done. The song was "Pantaloons" as performed by Tape Five, Aerophon Mix. The guys dressed in 1920s garb complete with sleeve garters. The ladies were gorgeous flappers with short, fringed, eye-catching dresses.

The routine went well, and I experienced a joyous sense of relief when it was over. However, I don't know if I'll ever do another quickstep. But on the positive side, what would we ever do without muscle memory?

Recommended background music: "Opus 1" as performed by the USAF Airmen of Note.

Storm Dance

Bolero, the Dance of Passion, Part 2

They capture and enchant, as inspiring and alluring as a thunderstorm's awe and majesty gliding across a steamy summer sky. Their power and presence cannot be denied, for they thrill and delight, muddling all other thoughts within their sway.

> *The bolero's first notes have their way with the dancers, enticing them. The music also captures and enchants—a seduction of Latin rhythm, a song of passion, demanding that desires be quenched.*

Her eyes are alive and invite, a soft, silvery passage to her very being, revealing the tempos and melodies of her life. He finds himself a willing prisoner, adrift in their surreal hue, exciting yet soothing.

> *He leads her through the dance, surrendering to her conjurement of lyrical, pale blue and enthralled by the dance's unmistakable mystique. She too feels his enchantment, his excitement—both dancers now spellbound, desperate, but rapt.*

The light plays with these jewels, a quiet and cool aquamarine at times, but more so a rich and sultry blue, somewhere between sea and sky, dawn and twilight, enhancing the music's mood—a storm-swept spell embraces.

The music's power is relentless—for magical moments, hearts pound and imaginations paint scenes of private pleasures. Hands stroke, and arms hold, legs brush, and hips press together sparking an already torrid tryst.

The music ebbs and entwined bodies sigh. The dance, the exquisite enticement ends. Gazes are lowered, and hearts calm. The adventure of the senses subsides.

The spell is broken but not forgotten. They know they will encounter this journey of sight, sound, and touch again and savor it again. Whenever they hold each other and he sees her eyes, whenever the bolero plays, they glide over the floor and are swept away by another ... storm dance.

Inspiration

There are times when you *must* look at your partner, when you can't take your eyes away, moments to enjoy, never forget, and perhaps write about.

Recommended background music—three powerful and gorgeous boleros: the emotion and sensuality of "Siente Mi Amor" as performed by Salma Hayak from *Once Upon a Time in Mexico*, you can feel the tropics with "Taboo" as performed by Les Baxter, Jojo Effect Remix, and the haunting and dynamic "Zaira" as performed by Astyplaz.

Motion

Dance Heat, the Rumba, Part 2

The way she moved her body, her hips, she gave new meaning to three simple words—slow ... quick, quick, slow ... quick, quick, slow.

Inspiration

Lynda was demonstrating Cuban motion during a class. It was mesmerizing!

Recommended background music: you must rumba to "Belle Chitarra" as performed by Andy Fortuna Production and "Wicked Game" as performed by Chris Isaac.

Pilot and Dancer

Dance Flight, the Waltz, Part 2

Silver wings earned in the summer of life, in the winter of '70, and onto Asian jungles, paddies, and mountains.

Silver wings earned in the autumn of life, in 2011, in studios and in American dance palaces.

Silver wings inspired by stars and stripes, beneath thumping rotor blades, above the din and fury of battle.

Silver wings inspired by music, floating across lustrous dance floors to the sound of beautiful three-four music.

Silver wings in a place of war and death, in combat flight's chaos and fright.

Silver wings in a place of music's life and its touch, with dance flight's hold and joy.

Silver wings with dedicated and skilled aircrews wearing olive drab, the loss of friends and comrades.

Silver wings while holding ladies in golden gowns, in the company of new friends and so many dances.

Silver wings attacked, with injury and scars, with
unseen wounds and the horrors of battle that haunt.

Silver wings with lingering pain and a lasting limp,
but ways to cope, overcome, and succeed.

Silver wings from the age of nineteen, now displayed
with awards and photos, but still with demon dreams
at night.

Silver wings at the age of sixty-one, now with every
step and every dance and sweet memories that abound.

Silver wings, from the guidance and care of knowing
veterans, protective and experienced.

Silver wings from the guidance and love of a knowing
teacher, talented and passionate.

Two lives, separate and apart, yet two lives very
much in common—bound by the silver wings of ... a
pilot and dancer.

Inspiration

Yes, this is a strange title for a verse in a book primarily
about ballroom dancing. But this odd coupling has
everything to do with my life's many transitions: from
high school student to US Army flight student; then

in combat as a helicopter pilot in Vietnam to inner-city school teacher, labor advocate, and union official; through PTSD's devastation, counseling, and recovery; the daily challenges of family and parenting; numerous physical set-backs—surviving all to eventually write and dance.

I love the fact that I have earned two sets of silver wings—the first in February 1970 with my warrant-officer bars. Mom pinned my bars on, and Dad pinned my wings on. The second when Lynda showed me dance flight with a waltz in May 2011. We both wear small sterling rings in the shape of wings to remember that moment.

On a personal note, Dad was a crew chief on US Marine Corps F-4U Corsairs in World War II in the Pacific theater. And in March 2015, my daughter, Jacqueline Noelle, completed flight-attendant school, and I pinned on her wings—what a thrill that was. It seems wings run in the family.

Recommended background music: "Balkan Melody" as performed by Bert Kaempfret and His Orchestra, "Vito's Waltz, the Godfather" as performed by the Tuxedo Junction Band and "Volare" as performed by Bobby Rydell, which has the best dance-ability. Note that in Italian *volare* means "to fly."

Part 4

The Ladies

Beauty and the Dance, Part 2

When dancing, there are times when the eyes are closed, stolen seconds for taking in the beauty of touch and sound—sublime moments with music and partner.

Then, when the eyes open, those moments become enhanced by the beauty of sight—the dancer in your arms, the reason, of course, for dancing.

Inspiration

During a private lesson, Lynda and I were dancing a bolero. My balance was on, the song was a favorite, and I had just conquered a new step—the dance felt perfect. I closed my eyes just to take in the moment's sound and touch, and, of course, the beauty of sight was fulfilled upon opening my eyes.

Recommended background music: Lynda and I were dancing to "Eden" as performed by Sarah Brightman.

When All Else Fails

I watched her dance, this lovely lady. She saw me watching her dance. I watched her as she returned to her table. Again, she saw me watching.

I glanced away, avoiding eye contact—she did the same. I thought, wondered, hoped. The lovely lady sat quietly, wondering who knows what.

I walked toward her thinking, *What should I say?* She saw me approaching. I stumbled on the rug. *Now she knows I'm a klutz.* She placed her hand over her mouth to hide a smile.

What do I say? C'mon—think of something! The lovely lady glanced away and sipped her drink. I stood at her side and leaned in close to her. She looked at me and smiled.

I extended my hand and said, "Would you like to dance?" She took my hand, and I led the lovely lady onto the dance floor for our first dance.

That was easy, I thought. Yeah, just ask the lovely lady to dance when you don't know what to do, when you can't think of anything else, when you don't know what to say ... *when all else fails*.

Inspiration

I was watching a brand new leader at his first dance—he was nervous. I knew that just being at the dance was an act of personal courage for him. I don't know what was going through his mind or what he said, but he did dance with several lovely ladies.

Recommended background music: "Dance with Me" as performed by Michael Bolton.

Dance Flower

Spin the lovely lady, unfolding her gossamer dress. Watch as *they* blossom, becoming one beautiful ... *dance flower*.

Inspiration

I was watching several ladies dance, and as they spun, their dresses flared, forming delightful blossoms on the dance floor.

Recommended background music: the classic cha-cha, "Cherry Pink and Apple Blossom White" as performed by Perez Prado and "Tango Delle Rosa" as performed by Achille Togliani.

Secret Dancer

I've always wondered, hoped we would dance. I've always desired, wanted you in my arms. I've always danced with you in my thoughts and in my dreams. You remain my ... *secret dancer*.

Inspiration

Who doesn't have a secret dancer, or maybe secret dances?

Recommended background music: "Romance Anonyme" as performed by Ray Hamilton Orchestra.

Part 5

Final Thoughts

Magic Dance, Part 2

There is that special song for that special dance. Its melody is as memorable as it is evocative. Its rhythm and tempo guide us through a dance floor's foreplay. The lyrics express words of the heart and the mind, of desire and need.

This music is meant for you and me, will always be for you and me. This music is much more than the unison of a song's elements—it is more than a bond of movement and melody. It is an expression of love and understanding.

Wherever we are, whenever it plays, we will respond, simply move to the floor with words unspoken. We will join in our dance embrace and become romance in motion, enjoying the music, ourselves ... and our *magic dance*.

Inspiration

A continuation of "Magic Dance," whose focus is on the aftermath of the dance, this verse is more about the music's effect on the couple during the dance.

Recommended background music: "Magic" as performed by Olivia Newton John.

Dance Glow

Is she relaxed, following you with ease? Does she move with you? Does she look at you, watch you, smile, or sing a few lyrics? If so, she's enjoying your lead.

Does she style freely? Does she touch your cheek, shoulders, or neck with the music? Does she hold frame but press closer to your body? If so, she wants to be there in your arms.

Do you know her favorite dance and what steps she likes, and do you want to hear her giggle after them? Does she say, "Oh, I love that move," and ask you to repeat it? If so, you appreciate one another and are truly dancing together.

And after the dance, does she hug you, still cling to your arm as you leave the floor? Does she thank you and compliment you, saying, "Oh, very nice"? If so, you have touched her.

Does she recall your previous dances and say, "I love dancing with you. Come get me again"? If so, you have given her a gift—the gift of ... *dance glow*.

Inspiration

Special ladies and special dances make for unforgettable encounters on the ballroom floor. Their gift to me is more than the dance—it continues with the aftermath.

Recommended background music: "That's What You Do to Me" as performed by Colin James and the Little Big Band.

Save the Last Dance for Me

A last chance for making a dance memory, to say thank you for a lovely evening and even lovelier dances.

For the one you enjoy dancing with the most, the one who made you laugh and thrilled you earlier that evening.

To be with the one you just met and would like to meet again, to be with an old friend reunited after a long while.

An opportunity to compliment, to speak private words because something is on your mind, to ask out.

Because it's a tradition to be carried forth, the way every dance should end, the way it has to be.

For the boyfriend and girlfriend, or for a first date that went well, with hopes of another.

For husbands and wives with anniversaries, for the couple newly engaged awaiting their wedding day.

To embrace your lover, the one you share a life with and no other, to express words of romance and desire.

For long gazes and gentle touches, for taking in a fragrance, for a beautiful moment that should not end, to kiss.

To have you near, in my arms, and wanting you to know that I like you, adore you, I love you.

So we can become partners while the final song plays, closer than anyone else on the floor—so many reasons ... to *save the last dance for me.*

Inspiration

In my experiences, going back to when I played in a band with my brothers, the last dance was always meaningful and special and reserved for someone special.

Recommended background music: "Vaya Con Dios" as performed by Julio Iglesias.

Reflections

The evening is spent, and the hall is clearing, the dances were many, and the music is done on this extraordinary night. Now shoes are being changed and glasses emptied. We thank the DJ and hostess and make our goodbyes. The body says it's tired and needs to rest, and the mind is satisfied but reflects.

The new dancers are improving and enjoying themselves and new friends. Seasoned dancers welcome, help, and encourage them. Good news about an opportunity for our teacher and a student's accomplishment enhanced the evening with excitement, congratulations, and toasts.

I danced a new step in the waltz, but it wasn't smooth —needs more work, but the teacher will fix that. My foxtrot felt just fine, and the tempo was perfect. It's hard to beat Sinatra tunes.

A truly romantic rumba passed too quickly. Confidence is returning to my tango even though I lost balance and stumbled. The lady didn't mind—she understood, and it still felt wonderful.

One cha-cha wasn't too fast so I attempted more intricate moves that my partner followed without effort. My samba is coming along, and two new steps in foxtrot brought needed variety—the same for my bolero.

The single-time swing was memorable, and much practicing of the toe-heel-cross has paid off. One east-coast tune reached out and grabbed us—the dance of the night.

The ladies, oh, the ladies. One born to bolero, another born to foxtrot, while others improve with every lesson and every dance, feeling the music and letting go to follow their newly found passions.

Such was the evening with good music and dancing and their pleasures, shared with good friends. All went well on the floor, and now all is committed to memory for review and such delightful ... *reflections*.

Inspiration

This was an exceptional evening of dance, a Halloween party at Avon Oaks Ballroom in Girard, Ohio, with so many memorable experiences as both participant and observer. I'm so lucky that there are such beautiful people in my dance community who love to share dance.

Recommended background music: "When I Leave Here" as performed by Robben Ford.

Learning the Last Step

Learning the last step shall not come to be—dance is infinite.

Inspiration

You never stop learning! How many times throughout your life have you heard that adage? It's especially true with ballroom dancing.

Recommended background music: "Dance Me to the End of Love" as performed by Leonard Cohen.

Now remember—it's not too late to start dancing. Get on the floor, and have the time of your life! Dance!